Table of Contents

PETER AND KHOMOTJO PETER MASHITA

Address:
South Africa, 0700 Polokwane, 0742 Seshego zone6 109,
St Khensani drive 247
Phone: 0725438106
Email: khomotjomashita@gmail.com
Website: N/A
Title: Predestined Life: God's will
Book Genre: Non-Fiction
Author: Khomotjo Peter Mashita
Self-Published
About the Author:
Khomotjo Peter Mashita is a South African Christian author and entrepreneur who share his faith through his writing. His latest book, Predestined Life and God's will: teaches readers predestination and God's plans about their lives.

Predestined Life and God's will, is a powerful exploration of predestination and its role in shaping our lives.

Throughout the book, Mr Mashita references key biblical passages that support his teachings on predestination and the importance of living a purposeful life. He encourages readers to deepen their relationship with God and to seek guidance and strength from Him as they navigate life's challenges.

Mr Mashita's writing is deeply spiritual, and he encourages readers to take a holistic approach to their lives, integrating their spiritual beliefs with their everyday actions. He emphasizes the importance of self-reflection, prayer, and a deepening of one's relationship with God in order to live a life that is aligned with our predestined purpose.

Overall, "Predestined Life and God's will is a thought-provoking and inspiring book that will resonate with readers seeking a deeper understanding of their faith and purpose in life. Whether you are a devout Christian or simply interested in exploring spiritual teachings, this book offers valuable insights and guidance on how to live a purposeful and fulfilling life in alignment with God's plan.

PREDESTINED LIFE

Predestined Life: God's will
By Khomotjo Peter Mashita

What is predestination?

Predestination is a biblical concept that refers to God's sovereign and predetermined plan for the salvation of individuals. According to biblical wisdom, predestination means that before the foundation of the world, God chose certain individuals to be saved and granted them eternal life through faith in Jesus Christ. This concept is found throughout the Bible, particularly in the writings of Paul the Apostle, who taught that believers were predestined to be adopted as God's children through Jesus Christ (Ephesians 1:5).

The idea of predestination also emphasizes the sovereignty of God, who has complete control over the universe and every aspect of human life. It acknowledges that God has a plan and a purpose for every individual, and that nothing can happen outside of His divine will. This concept is expressed in Romans 8:28, which says, "And we know that in all things God works for the good of those who love him, who have been called according to his purpose."

However, predestination does not mean that individuals do not have free will or the ability to make choices. Rather, it means that God's plan for salvation is not based on human merit or works, but on His grace and mercy. The Bible teaches that all have sinned and fall short of the glory of God (Romans 3:23), and that salvation is a gift from God, not something that can be earned through good deeds (Ephesians 2:8-9).

In summary, predestination is the biblical concept that God has a predetermined plan for the salvation of individuals, based on His sovereignty and grace, and not on human merit or works. It is a profound and mysterious doctrine that emphasizes the love and mercy of God, and should be approached with humility and reverence.

5

Introduction

As Christians, we believe that every life is predestined by God, according to his divine plan and purpose. This concept of predestination can be difficult to understand and accept, raising questions about the nature of God's sovereignty and the role of human free will.

In this book, " Predestined Life and God's will," we will explore the biblical basis for predestination and its implications for our daily lives. We will examine the complex relationship between God's sovereignty and human agency, seeking to understand how these seemingly opposing concepts can coexist in harmony.

Throughout the pages of this book, we will delve into key passages from the Bible that speak to the concept of predestination, including Ephesians 1:11, Romans 8:28-30, and Jeremiah 1:5. We will also explore how the concept of predestination has been understood throughout Christian history, from the teachings of Augustine to the Reformation and beyond.

But this book is not simply a historical or theological exploration of predestination. Rather, it is a practical guide for how we can understand and apply the concept of predestination to our daily lives as Christians. We will explore how the knowledge of predestination can give us confidence and assurance in the face of life's uncertainties and challenges. We will also examine how it can provide us with a sense of purpose and meaning in our lives, helping us to discern God's plan for us and to fulfill our unique calling.

Through personal stories, scriptural insights, and the perspectives of leading Christian thinkers and theologians, we will gain a deeper understanding of how predestination is woven into the fabric of our lives as believers. Our hope is that this book will leave you with a greater appreciation for God's sovereignty and a deeper sense of purpose and meaning in your own life.

The concept of predestination is a controversial and often misunderstood topic within Christianity. Some believe that everything in life is predetermined by God, while others believe in free will and the ability to make choices that shape our lives. In this chapter, we will explore the biblical basis for predestination and its implications for our lives.

Jeremiah 1:5 - "Before I formed you in the womb I knew you, before you were born I set you apart; I appointed you as a prophet to the nations."

The verse from Jeremiah 1:5 is one of the most powerful passages in the Bible that speaks to the concept of predestination. This verse shows that even before we were born, God had a plan for our lives. He knew us intimately and had a specific purpose for us.

God's foreknowledge and plan for Jeremiah's life did not depend on Jeremiah's abilities, but on God's sovereign choice. Jeremiah did not earn his calling as a prophet; it was given to him by God. This verse illustrates that God is in control of our lives and has a purpose for each one of us. Predestination is not a new concept in the Bible. Throughout Scripture, we see examples of God's sovereign choice and plan for individuals and nations. For example, God chose Abraham to be the father of a great nation and blessed him with descendants as numerous as the stars in the sky (Genesis 12:1-3). He also chose Moses to lead the Israelites out of Egypt (Exodus 3:10-12).

In the New Testament, we see that God predestined believers to be conformed to the likeness of His Son (Romans 8:29). He also predestined us to be adopted as His children through Jesus Christ (Ephesians 1:5). Some may argue that predestination takes away our free will and ability to make choices. However, Scripture shows that our choices are still significant and have consequences. In Deuteronomy 30:19, Moses tells the

Israelites to choose life or death, blessings or curses. Joshua 24:15 similarly states, "choose for yourselves this day whom you will serve."

God's plan for our lives does not negate our responsibility to make choices and live in obedience to Him. Instead, predestination reminds us that God is in control and has a purpose for our lives, even when we do not understand it.

Conclusion:

The concept of predestination may be challenging to understand and accept, but Scripture shows us that it is a biblical truth. God has a plan for each of our lives, and He knew us intimately before we were even born. Our choices still matter, but they do not change God's sovereign plan for us. As we trust in God's plan and purpose for our lives, we can find peace and security in knowing that He is in control.

So, join me on this journey as we explore the mystery of predestination and discover the ways in which it can transform our lives and deepen our faith in Christ.

Chapter 2: The Foreknown: Understanding God's Plan for Your Life

Have you ever asked yourself what your purpose in life is? Have you ever felt lost or confused about what direction to take? We all have at some point. But the good news is, God has a plan for each one of us. In this chapter, we will explore the concept of being foreknown by God and how that relates to understanding His plan for your life.

The Foreknown:

To be foreknown by God means that He knew you before you were even born. Jeremiah 1:5 says, "Before I formed you in the womb I knew you, before you were born I set you apart; I appointed you as a prophet to the nations." This verse shows that God had a specific plan for Jeremiah's life even before he was born. He knew his purpose and set him apart for a specific task.

We can also see this concept in the New Testament. In Ephesians 1:4-5, it says, "For he chose us in him before the creation of the world to be holy and blameless in his sight. In love, he predestined us for adoption to sonship through Jesus Christ, in accordance with his pleasure and will." God had a plan for us before the world was even created. He chose us to be part of His family and predestined us to be adopted as His children through Jesus Christ.

Understanding God's Plan:

So, how do we understand God's plan for our lives? First, we need to seek Him and His will. Proverbs 3:5-6 says, "Trust in the Lord with all your heart and lean not on your own understanding; in all your ways submit to him, and he will make your paths straight." We need to trust in God and submit to Him. This means putting aside our own desires and seeking His will for our lives.

Secondly, we need to be obedient to God's leading. We need to listen to His voice and follow where He leads us. Proverbs 16:9 says, "In their hearts humans plan their course, but the Lord establishes their steps." We can make plans, but ultimately, it is God who establishes our steps. We need to be obedient to His leading, even if it doesn't make sense to us.

Finally, we need to have faith in God's plan. Hebrews 11:1 says, "Now faith is confidence in what we hope for and assurance about what we do not see." We may not always see the full picture or understand God's plan, but we need to have faith that He knows what is best for us.

Conclusion:

Being foreknown by God means that He has a plan for each one of us. We need to seek Him and His will, be obedient to His leading, and have faith in His plan for our lives. As we trust in God and His plan, we will find purpose and fulfillment in our lives. Remember, God has a specific plan for you. Seek Him and His will, and He will guide you on the path He has set before you.

Chapter 3: Predestined for a Purpose: Finding Your Calling in Life

As human beings, we often ask ourselves what our purpose is in life. We wonder why we were created and what we are meant to do on this earth. It is a question that has been asked by many throughout history. The Bible, however, provides us with clear answers about our purpose and calling in life. In this chapter, we will explore what it means to be predestined for a purpose and how we can discover and fulfill that purpose.

Predestined for a Purpose

The Bible tells us that as believers, we have been predestined for a purpose. In Romans 8:29, we read that God foreknew us and predestined us to be conformed to the image of His Son. This means that before we were even born, God had a plan and purpose for our lives. He knew what He wanted us to become and what He wanted us to do.

Ephesians 1:5 also speaks about our predestination. It says that God predestined us for adoption as sons and daughters through Jesus Christ. This means that we were chosen by God to be part of His family and to inherit all the blessings that come with being a child of God.

However, it is important to note that not everyone is predestined for salvation. In Matthew 22:14, Jesus said that many are called but few are chosen. This means that while everyone is called to salvation, not everyone will choose to accept it.

Discovering Your Purpose

So, how do we discover our purpose and calling in life? Firstly, we need to understand that it is God who reveals our purpose to us. In Matthew 11:27, Jesus said that no one knows the Father except the Son and those to whom the Son chooses to reveal Him. This means that we cannot discover our purpose on our own, but we need to rely on God to reveal it to us.

John 6:44 also tells us that no one can come to Jesus unless the Father draws them. This means that it is God who initiates the process of calling us to fulfill our purpose. We cannot come to Him on our own.

Acts 13:48 further emphasizes this point. It says that as many as were appointed to eternal life believed. This means that it is God who appoints us to eternal life and also calls us to fulfill our purpose.

Fulfilling Your Purpose

Once we have discovered our purpose, it is important that we fulfill it. In Ephesians 2:5, we read that it is by grace that we have been saved and raised up with Christ to fulfill the good works that God prepared for us beforehand.

It is important to note that fulfilling our purpose is not always easy. We may face challenges and obstacles along the way. However, we can take comfort in the fact that God is with us every step of the way. He will provide us with the strength and guidance we need to fulfill our purpose.

In conclusion, as believers, we have been predestined for a purpose. We were chosen by God to be part of His family and to fulfill a specific calling in life. We cannot discover our purpose on our own, but we need to rely on God to reveal it to us. Once we have discovered our purpose, it is important that we fulfill it, even in the face of challenges and obstacles. May we always seek God's guidance and strength as we strive to fulfill the purpose for which we were created.

Chapter 4: The Role of Free Will in a Predestined Life

One of the most intriguing aspects of predestination is the relationship between God's sovereignty and human free will. It can be challenging to reconcile the idea that we have free will with the concept that our lives are predestined according to God's plan. However, as we will see, the Bible teaches that both of these concepts are true and work together in a beautiful and mysterious way.

In Matthew 11:27, Jesus declares, "All things have been handed over to me by my Father, and no one knows the Son except the Father, and no one knows the Father except the Son and anyone to whom the Son chooses to reveal him." This passage emphasizes the sovereignty of God, who has given everything into the hands of Jesus. However, notice that Jesus says that the Father has given Him the authority to reveal Him to whomever He chooses. This implies that, while God is sovereign, He has also given us the freedom to choose whether or not to receive the revelation of His truth.

Similarly, in Matthew 22:14, Jesus tells the parable of the wedding feast, where many are invited, but few are chosen. This passage highlights the fact that, while many are invited to come to the feast (representing the call of God), only a few are chosen. The chosen are those who respond positively to the invitation, indicating that they have exercised their free will to accept God's offer of salvation.

Romans 8:29 further emphasizes the idea that God's predestination is not at odds with our free will. It says, "For those whom he foreknew he also predestined to be conformed to the image of his Son, in order that he might be the firstborn among many brothers." This passage teaches that God has predestined us to be conformed to the image of Christ, but notice the phrase "whom he foreknew." This implies that God's predestination is based on His foreknowledge of who will choose to follow Him. He predestines those who will respond positively to His call, but He does not force anyone to do so.

So, what does all of this mean for our lives? It means that while God has predestined us according to His plan, He has also given us the freedom to choose whether or not to follow that plan. Our free will is not in conflict with God's predestination, but rather works together with it in a beautiful and mysterious way. As we exercise our free will to choose God, we become part of His predestined plan for our lives, conforming to the image of His Son and fulfilling the purposes for which we were created.

In conclusion, as we navigate the tension between God's sovereignty and human free will, we can take comfort in the fact that both are true and work together in a beautiful and mysterious way. We can trust that God's predestination for our lives is good and perfect, and we can exercise our free will to choose to follow His plan, becoming part of His predestined family and fulfilling the purposes for which we were created.

Chapter 5: The Paradox of Predestination and Human Responsibility

As we've explored the concept of predestination, we've seen that God has predestined our lives according to His plan, yet we also have free will and the responsibility to choose whether or not to follow Him. This paradox can be challenging to understand, but the Bible provides insight into how these two concepts work together.

One passage that speaks to this paradox is Philippians 2:12-13, which says, "Therefore, my dear friends, as you have always obeyed—not only in my presence, but now much more in my absence—continue to work out your salvation with fear and trembling, for it is God who works in you to will and to act in order to fulfill his good purpose." This passage teaches that we are responsible for working out our salvation with fear and trembling, yet it is also God who works in us to will and to act according to His purpose. We have the responsibility to choose to obey God, but it is only through His work in us that we are able to do so.

Another passage that speaks to this paradox is Romans 9:16, which says, "It does not, therefore, depend on human desire or effort, but on God's mercy." This passage emphasizes that our salvation does not depend on our own effort or desire, but rather on God's mercy. It is only through His grace that we are able to be saved, yet we still have the responsibility to respond to His call and accept His offer of salvation.

We also see this paradox in the story of Jonah. God had predestined that Jonah would go to Nineveh and preach to the people there, yet Jonah had the free will to choose whether or not to obey God's command. He initially chose to run away from God, but ultimately chose to obey and preach to the people of Nineveh, leading to their repentance and salvation.

So, what does all of this mean for our lives? It means that while God has predestined our lives according to His plan, we also have the responsibility to choose whether or not to follow Him. We cannot earn our salvation through our own effort or desire, but we must respond to God's call and accept His offer of salvation. It is only through His grace and work in us that we are able to obey Him and fulfill His purposes for our lives.

In conclusion, the paradox of predestination and human responsibility can be challenging to understand, but the Bible provides insight into how these two concepts work together. We are responsible for choosing to follow God, yet it is only through His grace and work in us that we are able to do so. As we navigate this paradox, we can trust in God's goodness and sovereignty, knowing that He has predestined us according to His perfect plan and will empower us to fulfill His purposes for our lives.

Chapter 6: The Power of Prayer in Discovering Your Predestined Life

As we've explored the concept of predestination and human responsibility, we've seen that God has a plan for our lives and calls us to follow Him. One powerful tool that we have to discover and fulfill this plan is prayer. Prayer allows us to connect with God, seek His guidance, and align our will with His.

One passage that speaks to the power of prayer is Matthew 7:7-8, which says, "Ask and it will be given to you; seek and you will find; knock and the door will be opened to you. For everyone who asks receives; the one who seeks finds; and to the one who knocks, the door will be opened." This passage teaches that when we come to God in prayer, He is faithful to answer and provide for our needs. As we seek His guidance and direction for our lives, He will reveal His plan and purpose to us.

Another passage that speaks to the power of prayer is James 5:16, which says, "Therefore confess your sins to each other and pray for each other so that you may be healed. The prayer of a righteous person is powerful and effective." This passage emphasizes the importance of prayer in our relationships with others and in our personal lives. When we come to God in prayer with a repentant heart and a desire to seek His will, He is faithful to heal and transform us.

In addition to these passages, there are many other examples throughout the Bible of the power of prayer in discovering and fulfilling God's plan for our lives. From the prayers of Abraham, Moses, and David to the prayers of Jesus and the early church, prayer is a consistent theme throughout Scripture.

So, what does this mean for our lives? It means that prayer is a powerful tool that we have to discover and fulfill God's plan for our lives. As we come to God in prayer, seeking His guidance and direction, He is faithful to answer and reveal His will to us. Prayer also allows us to align our will with His and to trust in His goodness and sovereignty.

In conclusion, the power of prayer is an essential aspect of discovering and fulfilling our predestined lives. As we come to God in prayer, seeking His guidance and direction, He is faithful to answer and reveal His plan and purpose for our lives. Let us embrace the power of prayer and trust in God's goodness and sovereignty as we seek to fulfill His predestined plan for our lives.

Chapter 7: Overcoming Obstacles on the Path to Your Predestined Life

As we seek to discover and fulfill God's plan for our lives, we will inevitably face obstacles and challenges along the way. These obstacles can take many forms, including personal struggles, external circumstances, and spiritual warfare. However, the good news is that God has given us the tools we need to overcome these obstacles and fulfill our predestined lives.

One passage that speaks to the importance of overcoming obstacles is Romans 8:37, which says, "No, in all these things we are more than conquerors through him who loved us." This passage reminds us that we are not alone in our struggles and that through Christ, we have the power to overcome any obstacle that comes our way.

Another passage that speaks to the importance of overcoming obstacles is James 1:2-4, which says, "Consider it pure joy, my brothers and sisters, whenever you face trials of many kinds, because you know that the testing of your faith produces perseverance. Let perseverance finish its work so that you may be mature and complete, not lacking anything." This passage emphasizes that the obstacles we face can actually strengthen our faith and character, leading us to become more mature and complete in Christ.

In addition to these passages, there are many other examples throughout the Bible of individuals who faced obstacles and challenges on the path to fulfilling their predestined lives. From Joseph and David to Paul and Peter, these individuals faced incredible challenges but ultimately overcame them through faith in God and His power.

So, what does this mean for our lives? It means that when we face obstacles on the path to our predestined lives, we must trust in God's power and strength to overcome them. We must persevere in the face of adversity and trust that God is using our struggles to refine and shape us for His purposes.

Overcoming obstacles is an essential aspect of fulfilling our predestined lives. As we face challenges and struggles, let us trust in God's power and strength to overcome them and lead us to fulfill His plan and purpose for our lives. Let us persevere in the face of adversity and become more mature and complete in Christ.

Chapter 8: Embracing the Unknown: Trusting God's Plan for Your Life

The idea of embracing the unknown can be frightening, particularly when it comes to our own lives. We often desire to have complete control over every aspect of our lives, to know exactly what will happen in the future and what steps we need to take to get there. However, as believers, we are called to trust in God's plan for our lives, even when we do not understand or know what lies ahead.

One passage that speaks to the importance of trusting in God's plan is Proverbs 3:5-6, which says, "Trust in the Lord with all your heart and lean not on your own understanding; in all your ways submit to him, and he will make your paths straight." This passage reminds us that we must trust in God with every aspect of our lives, even when we do not fully understand His plan or purpose.

Another passage that speaks to the importance of trusting in God's plan is Jeremiah 29:11, which says, "For I know the plans I have for you," declares the Lord, "plans to prosper you and not to harm you, plans to give you hope and a future." This passage reminds us that God has a plan for our lives, and it is a good plan that will lead us to prosperity and hope. There are many examples throughout the Bible of individuals who trusted in God's plan for their lives, even when it seemed impossible or unlikely. From Abraham and Sarah to Moses and Esther, these individuals chose to trust in God's plan and were blessed because of it.

So, what does it mean for us to embrace the unknown and trust in God's plan for our lives? It means letting go of our desire for control and surrendering our lives to God, knowing that His plan is far greater than anything we could imagine. It means being willing to take risks and step out in faith, even when we do not know the outcome.

Embracing the unknown also means being willing to wait on God's timing. In Psalm 27:14, the psalmist writes, "Wait for the Lord; be strong and take heart and wait for the Lord." This passage reminds us that we must be patient and wait on God's timing, trusting that His plan will unfold in the perfect way and at the perfect time.

Finally, embracing the unknown means seeking God's guidance and direction through prayer and studying His Word. In Psalm 119:105, the psalmist writes, "Your word is a lamp for my feet, a light on my path." This passage reminds us that God's Word is a guide for our lives and that through prayer and studying His Word, we can gain wisdom and direction for our lives.

Embracing the unknown and trusting in God's plan for our lives can be difficult, but it is essential for fulfilling our predestined lives. As we surrender our lives to God, let us trust in His plan and be willing to take risks and step out in faith. Let us be patient and wait on God's timing, seeking His guidance and direction through prayer and studying His Word. In doing so, we can embrace the unknown and experience the blessings of living out our predestined lives according to God's perfect plan.

Chapter 9: The Mystery of Predestination: Exploring God's Sovereignty

The concept of predestination has been a source of mystery and controversy for many centuries. Some believe that predestination implies that God has already predetermined our every action and choice in life, while others believe that predestination simply means that God has a plan and purpose for our lives. In this chapter, we will explore the mystery of predestination and delve deeper into God's sovereignty over our lives.

Ephesians 1:11 tells us that "In him we have obtained an inheritance, having been predestined according to the purpose of him who works all things according to the counsel of his will." This verse clearly shows that predestination is a result of God's plan and purpose for our lives. It is not a predetermined path that we are forced to follow, but rather a divine plan that we can choose to accept or reject.

Romans 8:28-30 further emphasizes the role of predestination in our lives, "And we know that for those who love God all things work together for good, for those who are called according to his purpose. For those whom he foreknew he also predestined to be conformed to the image of his Son, in order that he might be the firstborn among many brothers. And those whom he predestined he also called, and those whom he called he also justified, and those whom he justified he also glorified." This passage tells us that God works all things together for our good and that those whom he foreknew, he also predestined to be conformed to the image of his Son.

In light of these scriptures, we can conclude that predestination is a result of God's plan and purpose for our lives. However, this does not mean that we are without free will or that we are predetermined to follow a specific path in life. Rather, God's predestination works in conjunction with our free will to guide us towards the path that He has designed for us.

As we navigate through life, we will face many obstacles and challenges that may cause us to question God's plan for our lives. However, we must remember that God is sovereign over all things and that His plan for our lives is perfect. Isaiah 46:9-10 says, "Remember the former things of old; for I am God, and there is no other; I am God, and there is none like me, declaring the end from the beginning and from ancient times things not yet done, saying, 'My counsel shall stand, and I will accomplish all my purpose'"

Therefore, we can trust in God's plan for our lives, even when we do not understand it. We must have faith in His sovereignty and know that His ways are higher than our ways. Proverbs 3:5-6 says, "Trust in the Lord with all your heart, and do not lean on your own understanding. In all your ways acknowledge him, and he will make straight your paths."

In conclusion, predestination is a result of God's plan and purpose for our lives. It is not a predetermined path that we are forced to follow, but rather a divine plan that we can choose to accept or reject. We must trust in God's sovereignty over our lives and have faith in His plan, even when we do not understand it. We must remember that God works all things together for our good and that He will guide us towards the path that He has designed for us.

Chapter 10: The Comfort of Predestination: Finding Peace in Life's Uncertainty

Life is full of uncertainties. It is natural to feel anxious or stressed about the future, but as Christians, we have a source of comfort that the world cannot offer: the knowledge that we are predestined according to God's plan.

In Ephesians 1:11, Paul writes, "In him we have obtained an inheritance, having been predestined according to the purpose of him who works all things according to the counsel of his will." This verse reminds us that God's will is ultimately in control, and that we can find comfort in knowing that He is working all things according to His plan.

As we navigate life's uncertainties, we must remember that our ultimate purpose is to glorify God. In Romans 8:28, Paul writes, "And we know that for those who love God all things work together for good, for those who are called according to his purpose." This verse reminds us that even in difficult times, God is working all things together for our good and His glory.

We can find further comfort in the promise of eternal life. In John 10:27-28, Jesus says, "My sheep hear my voice, and I know them, and they follow me. I give them eternal life, and they will never perish, and no one will snatch them out of my hand." As believers, we can rest in the assurance that our salvation is secure in Christ.

Despite the comfort that predestination offers, we may still struggle with anxiety or fear about the future. In Philippians 4:6-7, Paul offers a solution: "Do not be anxious about anything, but in everything by prayer and supplication with thanksgiving let your requests be made known to God. And the peace of God, which surpasses all understanding, will guard your hearts and your minds in Christ Jesus."

Through prayer and thanksgiving, we can find peace in the midst of uncertainty. This peace comes not from our circumstances, but from our trust in God's sovereignty and plan for our lives.

In conclusion, the knowledge of predestination offers us great comfort in the midst of life's uncertainties. We can rest in the assurance that God is working all things together for our good and His glory. We can find peace in prayer and thanksgiving, trusting that God's plan is ultimately for our benefit.

Chapter 11: Predestined for Greatness: Unlocking Your Potential in Life

God has a plan for each and every one of us, and that plan includes greatness. It is easy to get lost in the day-to-day struggles and forget that we were created with a purpose in mind. But when we understand and embrace God's plan for our lives, we can unlock our potential and achieve greatness.

Jeremiah 1:5 tells us, "Before I formed you in the womb I knew you, before you were born I set you apart; I appointed you as a prophet to the nations." This verse reminds us that God knew us before we were even born and had a plan for our lives. We were created with unique talents, abilities, and passions that are all part of God's plan for us.

Psalm 37:23-24 says, "The Lord makes firm the steps of the one who delights in him; though he may stumble, he will not fall, for the Lord upholds him with his hand." As we walk in obedience to God's plan for our lives, He guides our steps and keeps us from falling. Even when we stumble, He is there to pick us up and help us keep moving forward.

Peter 2:9 says, "But you are a chosen people, a royal priesthood, a holy nation, God's special possession, that you may declare the praises of him who called you out of darkness into his wonderful light." We are chosen by God, set apart for a special purpose. We are royalty, and as such, we are called to declare the praises of God and to live a life that brings Him glory.

When we embrace God's plan for our lives, we can unlock our potential and achieve greatness. We can use our unique talents and abilities to make a difference in the world and to bring glory to God. We must trust in Him, seek His guidance, and walk in obedience to His will.

In this chapter, we will explore what it means to be predestined for greatness and how we can unlock our potential to achieve the purpose that God has for our lives. We will look at examples from the Bible of those who embraced their calling and achieved greatness, and we will explore practical steps that we can take to unlock our potential and achieve greatness in our own lives.

So, how can we unlock our potential and achieve predestined greatness? First and foremost, we must seek God and His plan for our lives. This means spending time in prayer and reading the Bible, so we can understand God's will for us. We must also embrace our unique gifts and talents, and use them to serve others and bring glory to God.

It's also important to surround ourselves with positive influences and mentors who can help us grow and develop our potential. We should seek out opportunities to learn and expand our skills, and be open to feedback and constructive criticism.

Finally, we must have faith and trust in God's plan, even when things get difficult. We may face setbacks and challenges, but we must believe that God has a purpose for everything and that He will use our struggles to strengthen us and ultimately lead us to our predestined greatness.

In conclusion, we are each predestined for greatness and have been created with a unique purpose in mind. By seeking God's plan for our lives, embracing our gifts and talents, and having faith in His plan, we can unlock our potential and achieve the greatness we were meant to attain.

Chapter 12: The Predestined Family: Understanding God's Plan for Your Loved Ones

As we journey through life, we are not alone. We have families that are chosen for us by God. Families are a gift from God, and He has a plan for each of our families. This chapter will explore the concept of the predestined family and how we can better understand God's plan for our loved ones.

The Bible tells us that God has a plan for our families, and that plan is predestined. In Jeremiah 1:5, God says, "Before I formed you in the womb I knew you, before you were born I set you apart; I appointed you as a prophet to the nations." This verse tells us that even before we were born, God had a plan for our lives, and that plan includes our families.

Psalm 127:3-5 says, "Behold, children are a heritage from the Lord, the fruit of the womb a reward. Like arrows in the hand of a warrior are the children of one's youth. Blessed is the man who fills his quiver with them! He shall not be put to shame when he speaks with his enemies in the gate." This verse tells us that children are a blessing from God, and that they are like arrows in the hand of a warrior. A warrior needs to know how to aim and shoot his arrows effectively, and so too, we need to know how to raise and guide our children in the way of the Lord.

In 1 Peter 2:9, we are called "a chosen race, a royal priesthood, a holy nation, a people for his own possession." This verse tells us that as Christians, we are a part of God's family. We are chosen and set apart by God, and we are called to be a holy nation.

God's plan for our families is not just about us, but it's about the generations that come after us. In Deuteronomy 6:6-7, God instructs parents to teach their children His commandments, saying, "And these words that I command you today shall be on your heart. You shall teach them diligently to your children, and shall talk of them when you sit in your house, and when you walk by the way, and when you lie down, and when you rise."

God's plan for our families is not always easy, and we may face challenges and difficulties along the way. But we can trust in God's plan, knowing that He is with us and He will never leave us nor forsake us (Hebrews 13:5). We can pray for our families and ask God to guide us as we raise our children and support our loved ones.

As we have previously discussed, predestination is a biblical concept that can provide comfort and guidance in our lives. But predestination is not just about our individual journey; it also applies to our families. In this chapter, we will explore God's plan for our loved ones and how we can support them in fulfilling their predestined lives.

One of the foundational principles of predestination is that God has a specific plan and purpose for each of us. This includes our families. In Jeremiah 29:11, God says, "For I know the plans I have for you, plans to prosper you and not to harm you, plans to give you hope and a future." This promise is not just for individuals, but for families as well. We can trust that God has a plan for our loved ones, and that He will guide them on the path He has set for them.

As parents, we have a unique responsibility to help our children discover and fulfill their predestined lives. Proverbs 22:6 says, "Train up a child in the way he should go, and when he is old he will not depart from it." This verse reminds us that our role as parents is not just to raise our children to be good people, but to help them discover their purpose and calling in life. We can do this by praying for them, teaching them the Word of God, and encouraging them to seek God's will for their lives.

But what about our extended family members? How can we support them in fulfilling their predestined lives? One way is through prayer. In 1 Thessalonians 5:17, we are told to "pray without ceasing." This includes praying for our loved ones. We can pray for God's guidance and direction in their lives, for wisdom and discernment, and for protection from the enemy's schemes.

Another way we can support our loved ones is by being an example of a predestined life. We can demonstrate to them what it looks like to live a life surrendered to God's will and purposes. We can share our own experiences of discovering our predestined lives and encourage them to seek God's will for their own lives.

It's important to remember that God's plan for our loved ones may not look the same as our own plan for them. We may have our own desires and expectations for their lives, but ultimately, we must trust that God knows what is best for them. As it says in Psalm 37:5, "Commit your way to the Lord, trust also in Him, and He shall bring it to pass."

In conclusion, God has a plan for our loved ones just as He has a plan for us. As parents and family members, we have a responsibility to help them discover and fulfill their predestined lives. We can do this through prayer, teaching, and being an example of a predestined life. Let us trust in God's plan for our families and seek to support them in fulfilling their unique purposes.

Chapter 13: The Predestined Church: Exploring God's Plan for His People

As believers, we are part of a greater body known as the Church. The Church is not just a physical building, but it is a community of people who have been called out by God for a specific purpose. In this chapter, we will explore God's plan for His people and how we can play a part in fulfilling that plan.

The Purpose of the Church:

The Church was established by Jesus Christ Himself, and its purpose is to proclaim the Gospel message to the world and to make disciples of all nations (Matthew 28:19-20). It is through the Church that God's plan for salvation is made known to the world.

PREDESTINED LIFE

The Role of Believers in the Church:
As members of the Church, we have a responsibility to contribute to its growth and effectiveness. In 1 Corinthians 12:12-27, we see that each believer has been given a specific gift by the Holy Spirit for the benefit of the Church. We are called to use our gifts to build up the Church and to fulfill its purpose.

Unity in the Church:
One of the main challenges that the Church faces is maintaining unity among its members. In Ephesians 4:1-6, we are urged to live in a manner worthy of our calling, and to make every effort to keep the unity of the Spirit through the bond of peace. It is only through the power of the Holy Spirit that we can maintain the unity that God desires for His Church.

The Church as the Body of Christ:
In Colossians 1:18, we see that Christ is the head of the Church, and the Church is His body. This means that we are called to be His representatives on earth, and to continue the work that He began during His time on earth. As the body of Christ, we are called to love one another, to serve one another, and to bear one another's burdens (Galatians 6:2).

The Importance of Fellowship:
Fellowship is an important aspect of the Church, and it is through fellowship that we are able to encourage one another and to grow in our faith. In Acts 2:42-47, we see that the early Church devoted themselves to fellowship, and as a result, they experienced tremendous growth.

The Church as a Light in the World:
As members of the Church, we are called to be a light in the world and to share the love of Christ with those around us. In Matthew 5:14-16, Jesus calls us to be the light of the world and to let our light shine before others, so that they may see our good deeds and glorify our Father in heaven.

The Church is an important part of God's plan for His people, and as believers, we have a responsibility to contribute to its growth and effectiveness. By using our gifts, maintaining unity, and being a light in the world, we can fulfill the purpose that God has for His Church. Ephesians 1:22-23 says, "And God placed all things under his feet and appointed him to be head over everything for the church, which is his body, the fullness of him who fills everything in every way." This passage highlights the importance of the church as the body of Christ, with Christ as the head. The church is not just a human organization, but a divine organism with Christ as its source of life and authority.

God's plan for the church is also reflected in the book of Acts, which describes the birth and growth of the early church. In Acts 2:42-47, we see that the early church devoted themselves to the apostles' teaching, fellowship, breaking of bread, and prayer. They also shared everything they had and met together in homes and in the temple. This passage gives us a glimpse of the kind of community that God desires for his people. The church is not just a place for individual believers to receive spiritual nourishment, but it is also a place where believers can use their spiritual gifts to serve one another and to advance God's kingdom. In 1 Corinthians 12, Paul uses the metaphor of the human body to describe the unity and diversity of the church. Just as the different parts of the body have different functions but work together for the good of the whole, so too the members of the church have different gifts and roles but are united in Christ for the common purpose of building up the body of Christ.

God's plan for the church also includes its mission to the world. In Matthew 28:19-20, Jesus gives the Great Commission to his disciples to go and make disciples of all nations, baptizing them and teaching them to obey everything he has commanded. This mission is not just for the apostles, but for all believers, as we are called to be witnesses of Christ to the world (Acts 1:8).

The local church is a manifestation of the universal church, and God's plan for the local church is to reflect the same characteristics of the universal church. This includes a commitment to biblical teaching, fellowship, worship, prayer, and mission. The local church is also a place where believers can experience accountability, support, and encouragement as they live out their faith in the context of community.

In conclusion, God's plan for the church is a beautiful and multifaceted one. It is a plan that encompasses both the universal and local aspects of the church, as well as its spiritual and practical dimensions. As believers in Christ, we have the privilege and responsibility of being part of this plan, and we can trust that God will continue to build and grow his church until the day of Christ's return.

Chapter 14: Predestined for Salvation: Understanding God's Plan for Your Eternal Life

Salvation is a central theme in Christianity. As believers, we believe that we are predestined for salvation through faith in Jesus Christ. In this chapter, we will explore the biblical concept of salvation and what it means for our predestined lives.

Scripture References:

Ephesians 1:4-5 - "For he chose us in him before the creation of the world to be holy and blameless in his sight. In love he predestined us for adoption to sonship through Jesus Christ, in accordance with his pleasure and will."

John 3:16 - "For God so loved the world that he gave his one and only Son, that whoever believes in him shall not perish but have eternal life."

Romans 10:9-10 - "If you declare with your mouth, "Jesus is Lord," and believe in your heart that God raised him from the dead, you will be saved. For it is with your heart that you believe and are justified, and it is with your mouth that you profess your faith and are saved."

God's Plan for Salvation:

God's plan for salvation is based on His love for us. In Ephesians 1:4-5, we read that God chose us in Him before the creation of the world to be holy and blameless in His sight. This means that even before we were born, God had a plan for our salvation through Jesus Christ.

John 3:16 tells us that God loved the world so much that He gave His one and only Son, Jesus Christ, to die for our sins so that we can have eternal life. This sacrifice was made out of God's love for us, and it is through faith in Jesus Christ that we can receive salvation and eternal life.

Our Role in Salvation:

While God's plan for salvation is based on His love for us, our role in salvation is to have faith in Jesus Christ. In Romans 10:9-10, we read that if we confess with our mouth that Jesus is Lord and believe in our hearts that God raised Him from the dead, we will be saved. This means that we must have faith in Jesus Christ and acknowledge Him as our Lord and Savior in order to receive salvation.

The Comfort of Salvation:

One of the greatest comforts of salvation is the assurance that we have eternal life through faith in Jesus Christ. We do not have to fear death or worry about what will happen to us after we die because we know that we will be with God for all eternity.

In addition to the assurance of eternal life, salvation also brings us peace and joy. When we accept Jesus Christ as our Lord and Savior, we are reconciled to God and our sins are forgiven. This brings us great peace and joy, knowing that we are no longer separated from God by our sins.

In this chapter, we have explored the biblical concept of salvation and what it means for our predestined lives. We have seen that God's plan for salvation is based on His love for us and that our role in salvation is to have faith in Jesus Christ. We have also seen that the comfort of salvation comes from the assurance of eternal life and the peace and joy that comes from being reconciled to God. As predestined believers, let us embrace the gift of salvation and live our lives in faith and obedience to Jesus Christ.

Chapter 15: The Predestined World: Exploring God's Sovereignty Over Creation

As we delve deeper into the concept of predestination, we must also consider how it applies to the world around us. Is the world predestined to a certain fate, or do we have free will to shape our own destiny? The Bible tells us that God is sovereign over all creation and that He has a plan for the world, but what does that mean for us as His children?

In Genesis 1:1, we read, "In the beginning, God created the heavens and the earth." This verse tells us that God is the creator of all things and that everything in the world was created for His purposes. Psalm 24:1-2 reaffirms this, saying, "The earth is the Lord's, and everything in it, the world, and all who live in it; for he founded it on the seas and established it on the waters."

As we consider God's sovereignty over creation, we must also remember that the world is fallen and that sin has corrupted it. Romans 8:20-21 says, "For the creation was subjected to frustration, not by its own choice, but by the will of the one who subjected it, in hope that the creation itself will be liberated from its bondage to decay and brought into the freedom and glory of the children of God." This passage reminds us that the world is not perfect, but that God has a plan to redeem it.

In Ephesians 1:9-10, we read, "He made known to us the mystery of his will according to his good pleasure, which he purposed in Christ, to be put into effect when the times reach their fulfillment - to bring unity to all things in heaven and on earth under Christ." This passage tells us that

God's plan for the world is to bring unity under Christ, and that this plan will be fulfilled in His perfect timing.

As we consider God's sovereignty over creation, we must also remember that we have a responsibility to care for the world that God has entrusted to us. In Genesis 2:15, we read, "The Lord God took the man and put him in the Garden of Eden to work it and take care of it." This verse tells us that God has given us the task of caring for His creation and that we must be good stewards of the resources He has provided.

As we explore the concept of predestination, we must also consider God's sovereignty over creation. The world was created for God's purposes, and He has a plan to redeem it. We must also remember that we have a responsibility to care for the world and to be good stewards of the resources God has provided. As we trust in God's plan for the world, we can find peace in knowing that He is in control and that His purposes will be fulfilled.

As we delve deeper into the topic, we will see how God has a purpose for all of creation and how He is working all things together for the good of those who love Him.

God's Sovereignty Over Creation:

The Bible teaches us that God is the creator of the universe and everything in it. In Genesis 1:1, it says, "In the beginning, God created the heavens and the earth." This verse establishes God's sovereignty over creation, which means that He has complete control and authority over everything that exists.

Psalm 24:1 says, "The earth is the Lord's, and everything in it, the world, and all who live in it." This verse emphasizes the fact that God owns everything in creation, including us. Therefore, we must recognize that we are not our own but belong to Him.

In addition, Colossians 1:16-17 states, "For in Him all things were created: things in heaven and on earth, visible and invisible, whether thrones or powers or rulers or authorities; all things have been created through Him and for Him. He is before all things, and in Him, all things hold together." This passage affirms that God created everything for His purposes and that He is holding everything together.

God's Sovereignty and Our Predestined Lives:

God's sovereignty over creation is directly related to our predestined lives. Romans 8:28-30 says, "And we know that in all things God works for the good of those who love Him, who have been called according to His purpose. For those God foreknew, He also predestined to be conformed to the likeness of His Son, that He might be the firstborn among many brothers. And those He predestined, He also called; those He called, He also justified; those He justified, He also glorified."

This passage shows us that God has a purpose for our lives, and He is working all things together for our good. He knew us before we were born and predestined us to be conformed to the likeness of His Son, Jesus Christ. Therefore, our predestined lives are intimately connected to God's plan for creation.

Furthermore, Ephesians 1:11 says, "In Him, we were also chosen, having been predestined according to the plan of Him who works out everything in conformity with the purpose of His will." This verse emphasizes that God's plan for our lives is in conformity with His will, and He is working everything out according to that plan.

In conclusion, we see that God's sovereignty over creation is essential in understanding our predestined lives. He created everything for His purposes, and He is working everything together for our good. We must recognize that we belong to Him and that our lives are predestined according to His plan. Therefore, we must trust in His sovereignty and submit to His will for our lives.

Chapter 16: The Predestined Future: Understanding God's Plan for the End Times

As believers, it is important to have a proper understanding of the end times and God's plan for the future. The Bible speaks of a time when Jesus will return to the earth and bring about the culmination of all things. This chapter will explore the predestined future and provide insights into what we can expect in the end times.

One of the most important things to remember about the end times is that they are predestined by God. He has a plan for the future and has revealed much of it to us in the Bible. In Matthew 24, Jesus gave his disciples an overview of the end times and what would happen before he returned. He warned of wars, famines, earthquakes, and persecution. He also spoke of the rise of false prophets and the deception that would occur in the last days.

The book of Revelation also provides a detailed account of the end times, including the rise of the Antichrist and the tribulation period. It describes a time of great persecution and suffering for believers, but also promises that Jesus will return and establish his kingdom on earth. Revelation 21:4 says, "He will wipe away every tear from their eyes, and death shall be no more, neither shall there be mourning, nor crying, nor pain anymore, for the former things have passed away."

In addition to the biblical accounts of the end times, there are also many signs that we can observe in the world today that point to the coming of Jesus. The rebirth of Israel as a nation, the increase in natural disasters, and the rise of technology are just a few examples of how the world is aligning with what the Bible says will happen in the end times.

As believers, we must be prepared for the coming of Jesus and the end times. We must live our lives with an eternal perspective, knowing that our time on earth is limited and that Jesus could return at any moment. We must also share the gospel with those who do not know Jesus, so that they too can be saved from the coming judgment.

It is important to note that while the end times may be a time of great tribulation and suffering, as believers, we have the promise of eternal life with God. Romans 8:18 says, "For I consider that the sufferings of this present time are not worth comparing with the glory that is to be revealed to us." We can take comfort in the fact that God is in control of the future and that he has a plan for our ultimate redemption.

The predestined future is a time when Jesus will return and bring about the culmination of all things. It is a time of great tribulation and suffering, but also a time when believers will be saved and the kingdom of God will be established on earth. As believers, we must be prepared for the end times and live our lives with an eternal perspective, knowing that God is in control and that he has a plan for our ultimate redemption.

The book of Revelation is a key text in understanding God's plan for the end times. In this book, we see that God will judge the world, and that Jesus Christ will return to establish His kingdom on earth. The book also talks about the Antichrist, the tribulation period, and the final judgment.

In Matthew 24, Jesus himself spoke about the signs of the end times. He warned that there would be false prophets, wars and rumors of wars, famine, earthquakes, and persecution of believers. He also said that no one knows the day or the hour of His return, but that we should always be ready.

In 1 Thessalonians 4, Paul writes about the second coming of Christ. He says that the Lord will descend from heaven with a shout, and that those who have died in Christ will rise first. Then, those who are alive and remain will be caught up together with them in the clouds to meet the Lord in the air.

We can also see in 2 Peter 3 that God's timing is not like our own. Peter writes that a day is like a thousand years to the Lord, and that He is patient, not wanting anyone to perish, but everyone to come to repentance. He also says that the heavens and the earth are reserved for fire, and that we should live holy and godly lives, looking forward to the day of the Lord.

As believers, our role in the end times is to be faithful and obedient to God's commands. We should be actively sharing the gospel with others, living holy and righteous lives, and praying for the Lord's will to be done. We should also be prepared for His return, knowing that it could happen at any moment.

Ultimately, we can take comfort in the fact that God is sovereign and in control of the future. His plan for the end times is perfect, and we can trust that He will bring about His purposes in His perfect timing. As we look to the future, we should have hope and confidence in the Lord, knowing that He is faithful to His promises and that He will never leave us nor forsake us.

Chapter 17: Predestined to Suffer: Finding Meaning in Life's Painful Moments

Life is full of ups and downs. At times, we experience joy and happiness, but at other times, we encounter pain and suffering. Many people struggle to understand the purpose of suffering in their lives. However, as Christians, we can find comfort and hope in the knowledge that God has a plan for our lives, even in the midst of suffering.

Scripture tells us that suffering is not a new experience for humanity. Adam and Eve suffered the consequences of their disobedience in the Garden of Eden (Genesis 3:16-19). Job suffered greatly, but his faith remained steadfast (Job 1:20-22). The apostles suffered for their faith, but they considered it a privilege to suffer for the sake of Christ (Acts 5:41, Philippians 3:10).

The Bible also teaches us that suffering has a purpose in our lives. In this chapter, we will explore the concept of predestination to suffer and how it can help us find meaning in life's painful moments.

Predestination to Suffer:

As Christians, we believe in God's sovereignty over all things, including our suffering. We are predestined to suffer because we live in a fallen world (Romans 8:18-23). However, we can take comfort in the fact that God can use our suffering for His glory and our good (Romans 8:28).

PREDESTINED LIFE

One example of predestination to suffer is the life of the apostle Paul. He suffered greatly for the sake of the gospel, yet he considered it a privilege to suffer for Christ (2 Corinthians 12:9-10). Paul understood that his suffering was not in vain and that it had a purpose in God's plan for his life.

Finding Meaning in Suffering:

Although suffering can be painful and difficult to endure, it can also bring about growth and transformation in our lives. The Bible tells us that suffering produces perseverance, character, and hope (Romans 5:3-5). Through our suffering, we can learn to trust in God and rely on His strength to carry us through.

One way to find meaning in suffering is to view it as an opportunity to minister to others who are going through similar experiences. We can comfort others with the comfort we have received from God (2 Corinthians 1:3-4). Our suffering can also be a testimony to others of God's faithfulness and love.

Trusting in God's Plan:

When we are in the midst of suffering, it can be easy to question God's plan for our lives. However, as Christians, we can trust in God's sovereignty and His perfect plan for us (Jeremiah 29:11). We may not always understand why we are going through a particular trial, but we can have faith that God is working all things together for our good (Romans 8:28).

Predestination to suffer is a difficult concept to understand, but as Christians, we can take comfort in the fact that God is with us in our suffering. We can find meaning in our pain by trusting in God's plan for our lives and using our experiences to minister to others. As we persevere through trials, we can grow in our faith and become more like Christ. Let us turn to God in our times of suffering and trust that He will carry us through.

One of the key passages in the Bible that speaks to the idea of predestination to suffer is found in Romans 8:17-18, which says, "And if children, then heirs—heirs of God and fellow heirs with Christ, provided we suffer with him in order that we may also be glorified with him. For I consider that the sufferings of this present time are not worth comparing with the glory that is to be revealed to us."

These verses suggest that suffering is not something to be avoided or ignored, but rather it is something that we must embrace if we want to share in Christ's glory. This is not an easy concept to accept, but it is a powerful one that can bring great comfort and hope to those who are struggling with pain and hardship.

Another passage that sheds light on the idea of predestination to suffer is found in 2 Timothy 3:12, which says, "Indeed, all who desire to live a godly life in Christ Jesus will be persecuted." This verse makes it clear that suffering is a natural part of the Christian life, and that those who are committed to following Christ will inevitably face trials and difficulties.

But why would God predestine us to suffer? One possible answer is found in James 1:2-4, which says, "Count it all joy, my brothers, when you meet trials of various kinds, for you know that the testing of your faith produces steadfastness. And let steadfastness have its full effect, that you may be perfect and complete, lacking in nothing."

This passage suggests that suffering can actually be a tool that God uses to refine us and make us stronger in our faith. It may not feel pleasant in the moment, but if we can endure it with faith and perseverance, we will emerge on the other side with a deeper and more mature faith.

Finally, we can look to the example of Christ himself for insight into the concept of predestination to suffer. Philippians 2:5-8 says, "Have this mind among yourselves, which is yours in Christ Jesus, who, though he was in the form of God, did not count equality with God a thing to be grasped, but emptied himself, by taking the form of a servant, being born in the likeness of men. And being found in human form, he humbled himself by becoming obedient to the point of death, even death on a cross."

Jesus willingly suffered and died on the cross as part of God's plan for the redemption of humanity. His example shows us that even in the midst of great pain and suffering, there can be purpose and meaning if we are willing to trust in God's plan for our lives.

In conclusion, while the idea of being predestined to suffer is a difficult one, it is also one that can bring great comfort and hope to those who are struggling with pain and hardship. By embracing the concept of suffering as a tool for spiritual growth and maturity, we can find meaning and purpose in even the darkest moments of our lives.

Chapter 18: Predestined for Service: Understanding Your Role in God's Kingdom

As believers, we have been predestined for service in God's Kingdom. Our service is not only a responsibility but also a privilege to work with God in advancing His Kingdom. In this chapter, we will explore the nature of service in the Kingdom, the call to serve, and the empowerment to serve.

Service in the Kingdom:

The concept of service in the Kingdom of God is rooted in the life and teachings of Jesus Christ. Jesus came to serve and not to be served (Matthew 20:28). He demonstrated this through His life and ministry on earth, and as His followers, we are called to follow His example. Service in the Kingdom is not limited to any specific task or role. It is an all-encompassing call to serve God and others in every aspect of our lives. We are called to love our neighbors as ourselves and to use our gifts and talents for the glory of God (Matthew 22:37-40, 1 Peter 4:10).

The Call to Serve:

The call to serve in the Kingdom is not limited to a select few. It is a call that is extended to all believers. However, the call to serve may look different for each individual, as we all have unique gifts and talents that can be used for the advancement of the Kingdom.

God has a specific plan and purpose for each of us, and it is our responsibility to seek His will for our lives. As we seek Him, He will reveal the areas where He wants us to serve and the specific tasks that He has called us to do.

PREDESTINED LIFE

The Empowerment to Serve:
We cannot serve in our own strength. We need the empowerment of the Holy Spirit to be effective in our service to God and others. The Holy Spirit enables us to live a life that is pleasing to God and to be effective in the service that we have been called to do.

The empowerment of the Holy Spirit is not limited to a select few. It is available to all believers who are willing to submit to God's will and seek His empowerment. As we yield to the Holy Spirit, He will empower us to be effective in our service to God and others.

We have been predestined for service in God's Kingdom. Our service is not only a responsibility but also a privilege to work with God in advancing His Kingdom. As we seek God's will for our lives, He will reveal the areas where He wants us to serve and the specific tasks that He has called us to do. With the empowerment of the Holy Spirit, we can be effective in our service to God and others, fulfilling the purpose that God has predestined for us.

One of the key scriptures that speaks to our role in God's Kingdom is found in Ephesians 2:10, which says, "For we are God's handiwork, created in Christ Jesus to do good works, which God prepared in advance for us to do." This verse tells us that we were created with a specific purpose in mind - to do good works that God has prepared in advance for us.

Another important scripture that speaks to our role in service is found in 1 Peter 4:10, which says, "Each of you should use whatever gift you have received to serve others, as faithful stewards of God's grace in its various forms." This verse reminds us that we have been given gifts by God that are meant to be used in service to others.

Jesus himself exemplified the importance of service when he washed his disciples' feet in John 13:14-15. He said, "Now that I, your Lord and Teacher, have washed your feet, you also should wash one another's feet. I have set you an example that you should do as I have done for you." This act of humility and service was a powerful demonstration of Jesus' love for his disciples, and it shows us that service is an important part of our faith.

Service can take many forms, from volunteering at a local food bank to mentoring a young person to using our professional skills to help others. Whatever our specific calling may be, the key is to approach it with a servant's heart, putting the needs of others before our own.

In addition to serving others, we are also called to serve God. Romans 12:1-2 says, "Therefore, I urge you, brothers and sisters, in view of God's mercy, to offer your bodies as a living sacrifice, holy and pleasing to God - this is your true and proper worship. Do not conform to the pattern of this world, but be transformed by the renewing of your mind. Then you will be able to test and approve what God's will is - his good, pleasing and perfect will." This verse reminds us that true worship is not just about singing songs or attending church services, but it is about offering ourselves fully to God in service and obedience.

When we serve others and serve God with a willing heart, we not only fulfill our predestined role in God's Kingdom, but we also experience the joy and fulfillment that comes from living a purpose-driven life. May we all seek to discover and fulfill our unique calling through service to others and to God.

Chapter 19: Predestined for Love: Exploring God's Unconditional Love for His Children

The concept of predestination can often lead to questions and doubts about God's love for us. Some may wonder if God has predetermined their fate and whether they have any control over their lives. However, when we understand that predestination is about God's plan for our lives and not about our eternal destination, we can begin to see His love for us more clearly. In this chapter, we will explore God's unconditional love for us and how it relates to our predestined lives.

One of the most famous verses about God's love is found in John 3:16, which says, "For God so loved the world that He gave His only begotten Son, that whoever believes in Him should not perish but have everlasting life." This verse shows us that God's love is not based on our merit or worthiness but on His own character and nature. He loves us because He is love (1 John 4:8).

Another powerful scripture about God's love is Romans 8:38-39, which says, "For I am convinced that neither death nor life, neither angels nor demons, neither the present nor the future, nor any powers, neither height nor depth, nor anything else in all creation, will be able to separate us from the love of God that is in Christ Jesus our Lord." This verse assures us that nothing can ever separate us from God's love. No matter what we go through in life, His love for us remains constant and unwavering.

In Ephesians 1:4-5, we see that God's love for us is not just a general love for humanity but a personal and intimate love for each individual. It says, "For He chose us in Him before the creation of the world to be holy and blameless in His sight. In love, He predestined us for adoption to sonship through Jesus Christ, in accordance with His pleasure and will." This verse tells us that God chose us specifically and predestined us for adoption as His children through Jesus Christ.

God's love for us is not just a one-time event but an ongoing and active love that is constantly working in our lives. In 1 John 4:10, we read, "This is love: not that we loved God, but that He loved us and sent His Son as an atoning sacrifice for our sins." This verse reminds us that God's love is demonstrated through His actions. He sent His Son to die for our sins so that we could be reconciled to Him and have a relationship with Him.

As we navigate through life, we may face difficult times that can cause us to question God's love for us. However, we can be assured that His love is never-ending and that He is always with us. In Psalm 139:7-10, it says, "Where can I go from Your Spirit? Where can I flee from Your presence? If I go up to the heavens, You are there; if I make my bed in the depths, You are there. If I rise on the wings of the dawn, if I settle on the far side of the sea, even there Your hand will guide me, Your right hand will hold me fast." This verse reminds us that no matter where we are or what we are going through, God's love is with us.

In conclusion, God's love for us is a foundational truth that we must understand as we explore the concept of predestination. His love is not based on our performance or worthiness but on His own character and nature. He chose us specifically and predestined us for adoption as His children through Jesus Christ. His love is ongoing and active, constantly working.

Throughout the Bible, God's love for His children is a recurring theme. The apostle John, in particular, emphasizes this point when he writes, "See what kind of love the Father has given to us, that we should be called children of God; and so we are" (1 John 3:1 ESV). This love is unconditional and is not based on our performance or achievements but on God's grace and mercy.

The chapter explores different aspects of God's love, including His love as a Father, His love as a friend, and His love as a Savior. Through the life and teachings of Jesus Christ, we can see how God's love is sacrificial, selfless, and pure. Jesus showed His love for us by dying on the cross and paying the penalty for our sins. This is the ultimate expression of God's love for us.

Furthermore, the chapter emphasizes the importance of our response to God's love. We are called to love God in return and to love others as ourselves. The apostle Paul writes, "So now faith, hope, and love abide, these three; but the greatest of these is love" (1 Corinthians 13:13 ESV). Our predestined life is a life of love, and it is through our love for God and others that we can fulfill our purpose and destiny.

The chapter also explores the practical implications of God's love in our daily lives. It reminds us that we are not alone, and we have a heavenly Father who loves us unconditionally. We can find comfort, strength, and hope in His love, especially during difficult times. We are also called to share God's love with others, to be a light in the world and show compassion and kindness to those around us.

Other supporting scriptures for this chapter include Romans 5:8, which states, "But God shows his love for us in that while we were still sinners, Christ died for us," and 1 John 4:7-8, which says, "Beloved, let us love one another, for love is from God, and whoever loves has been born of God and knows God. Anyone who does not love does not know God, because God is love."

In summary, this chapter emphasizes the crucial role of God's love in our predestined lives as Christians. It reminds us of the depth, sacrificial nature, and practical implications of God's love for us and calls us to respond by loving Him and others.

Chapter 20: The Journey to Your Predestined Life: Steps to Take Today

As we come to the end of this book, we have learned that our lives are predestined by God, and that we have a purpose and a plan that God has prepared for us before the foundation of the world. However, understanding our predestined life is only the beginning. It is now up to us to take the necessary steps to fulfill our destiny and live the life that God has intended for us. In this chapter, we will discuss practical steps that we can take to journey towards our predestined life.

Step 1: Seek God

The first step to discovering your predestined life is to seek God. We must seek God with all our hearts, minds, and souls, and ask Him to reveal to us His plan and purpose for our lives. We can do this through prayer, fasting, reading the Bible, and attending church. As we seek God, He will reveal to us His plans for us, and we will gain a deeper understanding of our predestined life.

Scripture: "You will seek me and find me when you seek me with all your heart" (Jeremiah 29:13)

Step 2: Surrender to God

The second step is to surrender our lives to God. We must let go of our own plans and desires and submit to God's will for our lives. We must trust that God's plans for us are good and perfect, and that He knows what is best for us. We can do this by putting our faith in Him, and by obeying His commands.

Scripture: "Trust in the Lord with all your heart and lean not on your own understanding; in all your ways submit to him, and he will make your paths straight" (Proverbs 3:5-6)

Step 3: Develop a Personal Relationship with God

The third step is to develop a personal relationship with God. We must spend time with Him, talk to Him, and listen to Him. This can be done through prayer, reading the Bible, and attending church. As we develop a personal relationship with God, we will gain a deeper understanding of His plans for us and we will be able to discern His voice more clearly.

Scripture: "Draw near to God, and he will draw near to you" (James 4:8)

Step 4: Discover Your Gifts and Talents

The fourth step is to discover our gifts and talents. God has given each of us unique gifts and talents that He wants us to use for His glory. We can discover our gifts and talents through self-reflection, prayer, and seeking advice from others. Once we have discovered our gifts and talents, we can use them to serve God and fulfill our predestined life.

Scripture: "Each of you should use whatever gift you have received to serve others, as faithful stewards of God's grace in its various forms" (1 Peter 4:10)

Step 5: Be Obedient to God's Calling

The fifth and final step is to be obedient to God's calling. Once we have discovered our predestined life and the gifts and talents that God has given us, we must be obedient to His calling. We must be willing to step out in faith and follow His leading, even if it means stepping out of our comfort zone. We must be willing to take risks and trust that God will guide us every step of the way.

Scripture: "For we are God's handiwork, created in Christ Jesus to do good works, which God prepared in advance for us to do" (Ephesians 2:10)

Step 6

Seek wisdom and understanding from God: In Proverbs 3:5-6, it says, "Trust in the Lord with all your heart and lean not on your own understanding; in all your ways submit to him, and he will make your paths straight." Seek guidance from God through prayer and studying his word to gain wisdom and understanding about your purpose in life.

Step 7

Be willing to take risks: Sometimes, following your predestined life may require taking risks and stepping outside of your comfort zone. In Matthew 14:29-30, Peter took a risk by stepping out of the boat to walk on water towards Jesus. Even though he began to sink, Jesus was there to rescue him. Take the leap of faith and trust that God will be with you every step of the way.

Step 8

Build healthy relationships: Surround yourself with people who support and encourage you in your journey towards your predestined life. In Proverbs 13:20, it says, "Walk with the wise and become wise, for a companion of fools suffers harm." Seek out mentors, accountability partners, and friends who will challenge and inspire you to become the best version of yourself.

Step 9

Use your talents and gifts: God has given each of us unique talents and gifts to use for his glory. In 1 Peter 4:10-11, it says, "Each of you should use whatever gift you have received to serve others, as faithful stewards of God's grace in its various forms. If anyone speaks, they should do so as one who speaks the very words of God. If anyone serves, they should do so with the strength God provides, so that in all things God may be praised through Jesus Christ." Use your talents and gifts to serve others and fulfill your purpose in life.

Step 10

Persevere through challenges: On your journey to your predestined life, there will be challenges and obstacles to overcome. In James 1:2-4, it says, "Consider it pure joy, my brothers and sisters, whenever you face trials of many kinds, because you know that the testing of your faith produces perseverance. Let perseverance finish its work so that you may be mature and complete, not lacking anything." Trust in God and persevere through the challenges, knowing that he is with you every step of the way and that he has a plan for your life.

Remember, your predestined life is not something that is set in stone, but rather a journey of growth and discovery as you seek to fulfill God's plan for your life. Trust in him, seek his guidance, and take action on the steps that he reveals to you along the way. May God bless you on your journey to your predestined life.

Biography

"Predestined Life:God's will" is a groundbreaking book by South African author and entrepreneur, Mr Khomotjo Peter Mashita. With a deep understanding of spirituality and biblical teachings, Mashita offers a profound exploration of the concept of predestination and how it shapes our lives.

Through personal experiences and insights, Mr Mashita provides readers with a roadmap towards discovering their predestined purpose. He encourages readers to deepen their relationship with God, integrating spirituality with everyday actions, and reflecting on their lives in order to live a purposeful and fulfilling life.

"Predestined Life:God's Will" is an inspiring and thought-provoking book that is sure to resonate with readers of all backgrounds and beliefs. Mr Mashita's writing is powerful and engaging, and he draws heavily on biblical references to support his teachings.

Whether you are a devout Christian seeking to deepen your faith or someone interested in exploring spirituality, this book offers valuable insights and guidance on how to live a more meaningful and purposeful life. With "Predestined Life:God's will", Mr Khomotjo Peter Mashita has crafted a transformative guide that is sure to change lives and inspire readers to live a life that is aligned with God's plan.

PREDESTINED LIFE

Thank you for Reading...

* * *

Did you love *Predestined Life*? Then you should read *The African Warrior* by Khomotjo Peter Mashita!

The African Warrior

The story is about **Khomotso**, a child born with a pure strand of white hair on his right side and a mark on his right hand as prophesied in the heart of Africa. From a young age, Khomotso showed signs of great natural strength and a hunger for knowledge. He discovered a forbidden tree that granted him immense powers, which he used to become a renowned warrior and defend his people and land against other tribes and white colonizers. Khomotso was also a loving husband and father who trained his children to master their abilities. He became a legend in his own time and a symbol of strength and hope for his tribe. The story is set in Africa, a world of diverse cultures, traditions, and histories, where courage, strength, and family bonds are highly valued.

Witnessing his transformation from a young boy with great potential to a legendary warrior who defended his people and lands against all odds. We invite you to delve deeper into the world of "The African Warrior" and explore the diverse cultures, traditions, and histories that make Africa such a unique and fascinating place. With every page, you will discover new depths of meaning and relevance to our modern world. As you close this book, we hope you will carry Khomotso's message of strength, resilience, and hope with you wherever you go.